G. SCHIRMER'S EDITION OF SCORES
OF ORCHESTRAL WORKS AND CHAMBER MUSIC

SAMUEL BARBER

TWO SCENES FROM "ANTONY AND CLEOPATRA"

for Soprano and Orchestra

full score

1. "Give me some music"

2. Death of Cleopatra

G. SCHIRMER, Inc.

DISTRIBUTED BY

HAL•LEONARD®
CORPORATION

7777 W. BLUEMOUND RD. P.O. BOX 13819 MILWAUKEE, WI 53213

INSTRUMENTATION

1. "Give me some music"

Piccolo
Flute I
Flute II (changing to Alto Flute ad lib)
Oboe I, II
English Horn
Clarinet in B♭ I, II (II also in A)
Bass Clarinet
Bassoon I, II
Contrabassoon
Horn in F I, II, III, IV
Trumpet in B♭ I, II, III
Trombone I, II, III
Timpani
Percussion
    3 small untuned drums
      high, medium, and low
    Snare Drum
    Bass Drum
    Cymbals
    Tam-tam
    Triangle
    Antique Cymbals A, E
    Chinese bell-tree*
    Celesta
    Whip
Harp
Piano
Violin I, II
Viola
Violincello
Bass

*May be obtained from Carroll Musical
Instrument Service Corp.
209 West 48th St., N.Y.C.

Duration: 7 minutes, 45 seconds

2. Death of Cleopatra

Piccolo
Flute I, II
Oboe I, II
English Horn
Clarinet in B♭ I, II
Bass Clarinet
Bassoon I, II
Contrabassoon
Horn in F I, II, III, IV
Trumpet in B♭ I, II, III
Trombone I, II, III
Tuba
Timpani
Percussion
    Tam-tam
    Bass Drum
    Snare Drum
    Tenor Drum
    Cymbal
    Sizzle Cymbal
    Vibraphone
    Xylophone
Piano
2 Harps
Violin I, II
Viola
Violincello
Bass

Duration: 8 minutes

All instruments in the score are written in C

All rights of performance and broadcast are strictly reserved.

Orchestra parts may be obtained on rental from the publisher.

1

We are in Egypt in Cleopatra's palace. Antony has left for Rome and there are rumors. that he has married. The orchestral introduction portrays Cleopatra's fury when she demands the truth from a messenger and strikes him in her jealousy.

The music becomes more calm, recalling the tenderness of the lovers' separation. Bored, Cleopatra calls for music: "moody food of us that trade in love." She remembers how they first went fishing together when he called her "his serpent of old Nile." Her longing for him increases.

CLEOPATRA

Give me some music: music, moody
   food
Of us that trade in love . . . .
I'll none now!
Give me my angle, we'll to the river:
   there,
My music playing far off, I will betray
Tawny-finned fishes.
And as I draw them up,
I'll think them every one an Antony,
And say, "Ah,ha! y'are caught!"
That time — O times!
I laughed him out of patience; and that
   night
I laughed him into patience.
And the next morn ere the ninth hour
I drunk him to his bed:
Then put my crown and mantles on
   him,
While I wore his sword Philippan.
My man of men!
Charmian!
Give me to drink
   mandragora

That I might sleep out this great gap of
   time
My Antony is away.
My man of men!
O Charmian, where think'st that he is
   now?
Stands he, or sits he?
Or does he walk?
Or is he on his horse?
O happy horse, to bear the weight of
   Antony!
Do bravely, horse! for know'st thou
   whom thou movest?
The demi-Atlas of this earth.
He's speaking now, or murmuring:
"Where's my serpent of old Nile?"
(For so he calls me.)
Now I feed myself with most delicious
   poison.
Think on me,
That am with Phoebus' amorous pinches
   black,
And wrinkled deep in time . . .
Give me some music: music, moody
   food
Of us that trade in love.

Cleopatra has taken refuge in the pyramid after the defeat of her armies. Antony, who has stabbed himself, dies at her feet. The orchestra plays a funeral march as she decides to die with him. "Give me my robe, put on my crown," she commands and poisons herself by applying an asp which she has smuggled into the monument.

CLEOPATRA

Give me my robe, put on my crown, I
   have
Immortal longings in me. Now no more
The juice of Egypt's grape shall moist
   this lip.
Yare, yare, good Iras; quick, Methinks
   I hear
Antony call: I see him rouse himself
To praise my noble act.
Husband, I come:
Now to that name my courage prove my
   title!
I am fire, and air; my other elements
I give to baser life. So, have you done:
Come then, and take the last warmth
   of my lips.
Farewell, kind Charmian, Iras, long
   farewell.
Have I the aspic on my lips? Dost fall?
If thou and nature can so gently part,

The stroke of death is as a lover's pinch,
Which hurts, and is desired.
Come, thou mortal wretch.
(to an asp, which she applies to her
  breast)
With thy sharp teeth this knot intrin-
   sicate
Our life at once untie.
Peace, peace!
Dost thou not see my baby at my breast,
That sucks the nurse asleep?
As sweet as balm, as soft as air, as
   gentle —
O Antony! Nay, I will take thee too:
  (applying another asp to her arm)
What should I stay —
In this vile world?
Now I feed myself with most
   delicious poison
That I might sleep out
   this great gap of time.
My man of men!

It is suggested that this material be printed in programs accompanying performances, "By permission of the publisher G. Schirmer, Inc."

Two Scenes from "Antony and Cleopatra"

to *ORAZIO ORLANDO*

For Soprano and Orchestra

WILLIAM SHAKESPEARE

SAMUEL BARBER, Op. 40

I. "GIVE ME SOME MUSIC"

*: linger slightly

46378

ri - ver:__ there, My   mu-sic play -ing far off,_____   I will be-tray Tawn-y -finned fish -

And the next morn ere the ninth hour___ I drunk him___ to his bed:_____ Then put my crown and man-tles on him, While I

Fl.
Ob.
E.H.
Cl.1
I
Solo
p espr.
mp
Fl.2 change to Alto Flute
Solo
Give me to drink mandragora —
That I might sleep out — that great gap of time —
I
Vn.
II
p espr.
unis.
pp
Vla.
Vc.
13
Fl.1
1
Cl.
2
B.Cl.
espr.
f
Hn.
1
2
3
4
Solo I
mp espr.
Harp
— My An-to-ny — is a-way. —
My man — of
f espr.
p dolce
div.
unis.
pizz.
mf
Cb.

sits he? Or does he walk?_____ Or is he on his horse? O hap-py horse, to

bear the weight of An - to - ny! Do brave-ly, horse! for know'st thou whom thou

The de-mi At - -las of this earth.

He's speak - ing now, ___ or mur-mur-ing: "Where's ___ my ser - pent of old Nile?" (For

so_he_calls_____ me.)   Now_____ I

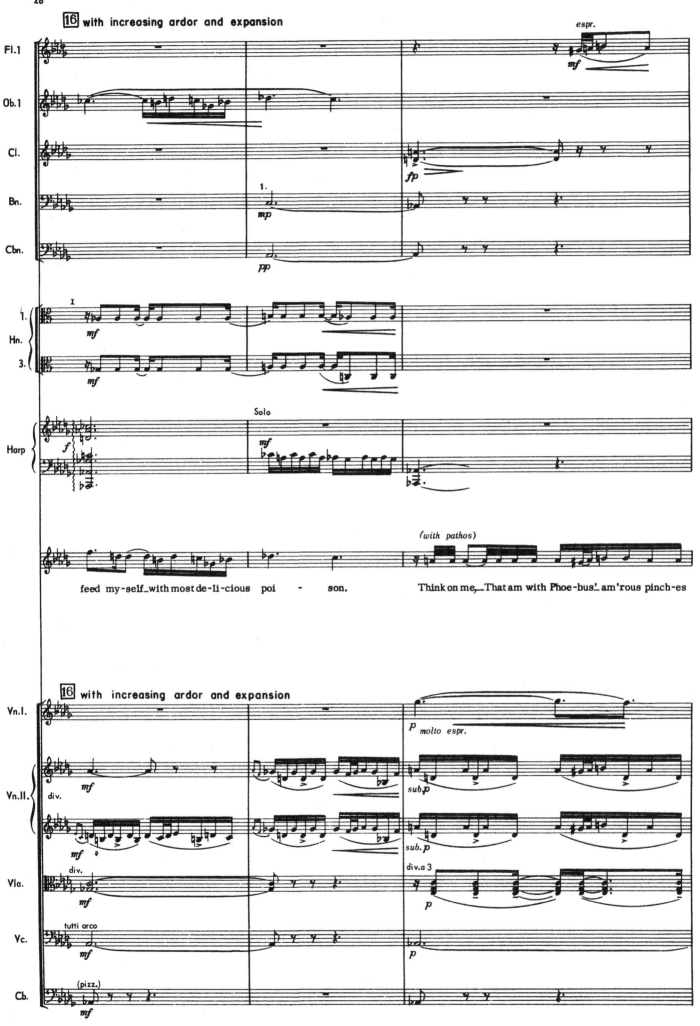

black,   And wrin-kled deep in   time . . . .

poco allarg.
a tempo
Picc.
Fl.
Cl.
Hn.
Perc.
Harp
con sord.
morendo
Tam-tam
— Of us — that trade in love. —
poco allarg.
a tempo
Vn.
Vla.
Vc.
Cb.
dolce
div.
pizz.

2. DEATH OF CLEOPATRA

46378

46378

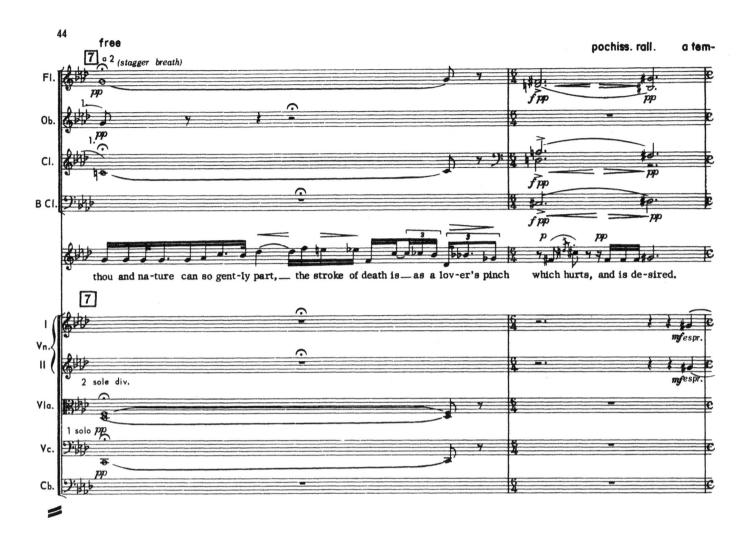

thou and na-ture can so gent-ly part, __ the stroke of death is __ as a lov-er's pinch which hurts, and is de-sired.

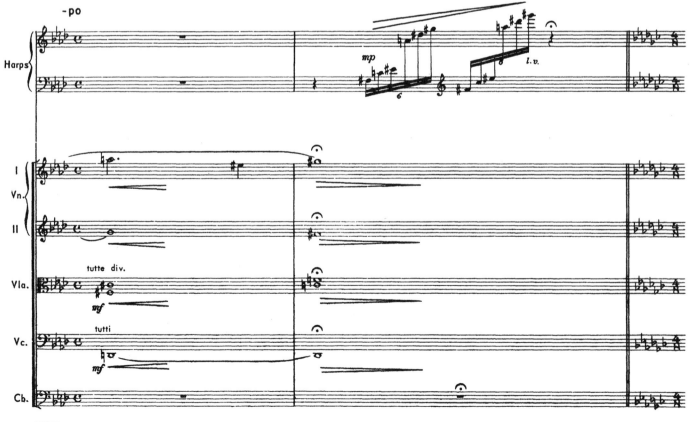

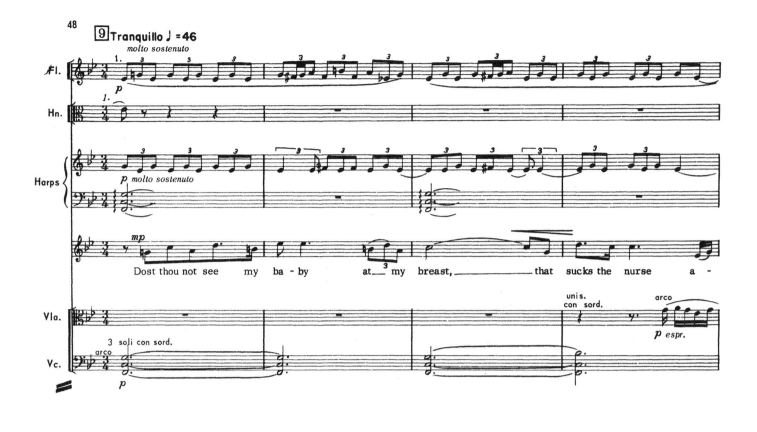

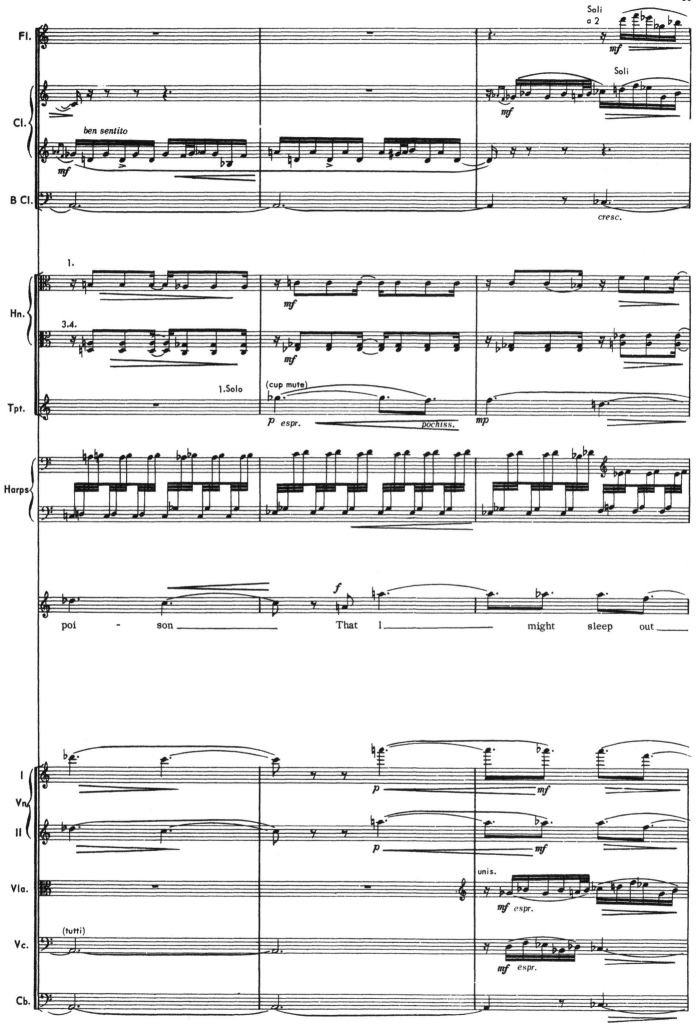

stringendo sempre di più